AN OTHERWISE PERFECT HISTORY

Poems
by

Julia Wendell

ITHACA HOUSE BOOKS

The Greenfield Review Press
Greenfield Center, NY

Grateful acknowledgement is made to the publications in which the following poems first appeared in somewhat different form:

The American Poetry Review: "Hypersomnia: Exhaustion After a Long Night's Rest"
The Antioch Review: "Possibilities"
Crazyhorse: "A Rope's Length"
The Greenfield Review: "Duet in the Suburbs," "Sometimes the Body's Unwilling"
Maryland Poetry Review: "Gray"
The Missouri Review: "Fireside"
Prairie Schooner: "Hatteras"
The Ohio Journal: "Entropy"
Quarterly West: "For You, Elizabeth," "Possibly So"
Southern Poetry Review: "Holding Pattern"

This book has been made possible, in part, through a literary publishing grant from the Literature Program of the New York Council on the Arts.

Cover photo, "Cabinet de curiosité" by Louis Jacques Mandé Daguerre. Reprinted with permission of the Collection de la Société Française de photographie.

PS
3573
E513
08
1986

Ithaca House Books
The Greenfield Review Press
2 Middle Grove Road
Greenfield Center, N.Y. 12833

AN
OTHERWISE
PERFECT
HISTORY

For Jack, my well-set lens

CONTENTS

Dust as we are, the immortal spirit grows
Like harmony in music; there is a dark
Inscrutable workmanship that reconciles
Discordant elements, makes them cling together
In one society. How strange that all
The terrors, pains, and early miseries,
Regrets, vexations, lassitudes interfused
Within my mind, should e'er have borne a part,
And that a needful part, in making up
The calm existence that is mine when I
Am worthy of myself!

--William Wordsworth, *The Prelude*

One:

Familial, Passed and Assumed

Fireside

All afternoon I listened to a fire,
wondering how its poor song was expired, sounding
like the long thin notes of a boy soprano, or a bird,
trapped in the great expanse between cathedral
windows. So a bird sings in my fire,
though its song has little to do with
the numerous birds that have filled our lives,
some made memorable in their own
flights into darkness. Little to do
with a boy who once trapped a sparrow,
then held a lit match to its wings to see if the bird
could save itself. It is November,
raining hard, and birds
must find shelter somewhere.
Mine has chosen a blue flame,
though it has no recollection of matches or burnt wings,
or of a small girl finding a few singed feathers
and approaching her brother with his crime.
No recollection of another mid-November,
or of a brother leading a sister to their father's greenhouse
to lay the small remains on a magnolia bush,
then turning to each other in that steamy greenery,
as he touches her plaid coat where the breasts should be,
telling her there is nothing to fear;
that there are only a few small burns
the purple flowers will heal, so come close
and the bird will be gone. Come close,
and the bird will fly through the greenhouse window
to the poplar tree and live
in the tree that is childhood,
until one day she lures it out
or burns it, quite unexpectedly,
in a fire.

Cat at the Window

Take a woman in a novel
who insults her man,
speaks of an endless fantasy which does not include him,
plucks a sickly carnation from his lapel,
then simply walks away.

Take another, more intimate scene: the mother
who tells her child not to cry when her pony
splits his belly open on a barbed wire fence.
Or take the old photograph of him the older child
still keeps pinned to her wall
in order to safeguard memory.

The way any scene comes back
like an unexpected snowfall. Or you,
undressing in the poor light
of a winter dawn with the cat
lying nonchalantly at his window.
Shifting lazily on his haunches
like an old man, he will wait out the day,
staring at the old oak out back
that won't let go its leaves.
Standing naked at the window,
you watch day come on and the trees, weary
with night. The squirrels surprise you
with their usual spitfire.
I see you turning, even now,
instructing me to come look at the neighbor cat,
chasing grizzled tails.
It is now full day. As it is

for the child just waking—
clutching the pony's picture,
she turns continually away from these scenes:
from her window, the driveway
and the one glazed eye of a doe slung over
the hood of her brother's '59 Ford. And she sees again

the angry eye of the mother who has just found
her daughter's dark fantasies postmarked
to an imaginary lover, the boy with the coaxing eye
who puts his hands to her breasts for the first time,
promising forgiveness. Now
the girl thinks little of forgiveness.
Though she will realize much later
that a departure is only
the first act of remembrance.
So the boy walks constantly out of memory.

Turning into the flat light of rain
toward the window (where oak leaves sag
under the weight), where in the present I will return
to myself, I choose to forget
the woman, the girl, the girl in me,
my letters, now fragments, spiralling in the chimney,
now lifting into black doves. I choose to forget the crystal
shattering, the door slamming,
still stammering against its wooden frame,
you turning continually away,
until even this scene
is the dust on dust of memory:
the way the cat sat at our window
all day through twilight,
and the way I catch him there, even now,
in these days after his death.

Holding Pattern

In these few moments of transit
(dawn rising from nothing
but a memory of itself) when those just waking
could be momentarily confused
about which half of the one-winged dial is in shadow,
a woman is soon to die in a room
where the scents of lavender soap and disinfectant
sicken a young girl. It's been days.
The girl's forced bedside vigilance is one hour
suffering into the next, shadows crossing
and uncrossing as the sun staggers
another ascent in fits and spurts.
Forgetting the girl and us, her other attendants,
in the white preoccupation of dying,
the woman rolls to one side and vomits whatever she can
into the stained porcelain bowl at bedside.

She believes
she has already known heaven.

In another part of the house
insects beat against a cupboard door.
A few escape as the girl is ordered
to find camomile tea to settle the stomachs
of the woman and her companions.
Most of the food has been spoiled.
We drink the tea anyway, as the day matures
into something none of us expects,
prolonged by its lack of faith
in anything but itself—
like a lover, who having loved too long
turns her naked self toward another,
feeling only the arrogant single-mindedness
of desire. Overhead

a jet, after circling for hours,
begins its descent into our neighborhood.

Sweeping across our lawn,
a crossed shadow.
Teacups rattle on their delicate saucers,
and we're scared—

losing grasp of the smallest thought to listen.

Elegy *In Absentia*

(for H.T.L. 1895–1985)

There is a hole in my attic
through which you flew two nights ago
into the December cold.
Though everyone knew at the time
you were still in Arizona and warm.
A shadow passed over your head.
You thought of clouds.
Is death more tender this way?

I will have to remember to patch that hole,
though most of my tools have been stolen
or are missing. First,
I will wait for spring to buy a ladder
and then learn to climb it, without you.

There is no simpler or more honest
way to say good-bye
than to continue the process of living
without regret or too many questions –
a process requiring faith,
in much the same way that the blind
learn to touch cold water
and envision blue.
I say this for my own mother,
born of you as I was not, who must now
cut the most delicate thread of all,
which is also blue,
and tuck it away in a box
labelled "last and most difficult
memories of you."

Please forgive us, those who were not there
to offer you water or to hear the words
that may have righted everything.
If I were blind, which I am not,
I would not be able to see

the hole in my house.
Would it be more painful
if I only felt the bitter cold,
in much the same way that death for you
was briefly felt,
but not seen, as a dark pressure
on your shoulder, directing
you toward an open door?

A Rope's Length

in memory of Frances Cole

The rains in Baltimore were not what I expected.
I expected taking some pleasure in a February,
cut off from snow, where I could only invent
the distant light of your city, a distant cold.
The two of us have something in common.
Our cities, their tenements, dusky commutes
to the suburbs, 5 o'clock sirens
trying to save God Knows Who. Our cities
dividing and dividing
like the cells dividing
terribly, within you.

I found it in the basement,
thick with dust, its heavy, seemingly endless coils —
a rope without function or give.
At the time I was sorting through old clothes,
through a few yellowed shirts with paper collars
as brittle as your letters
stacking up in a hatbox.

This weather began
with no warning, then
all morning fell too steadily.
I will remember it only by chance
because through it a neighboring tenement
has just caught fire.

Smoke braids itself downwind to me.
I stand at the basement door, the rope's
bitter end in my palm.
The Scarlatti you played
continues threading its way.

In one letter you told me of a man
who never asked your name
in the brief promises of a night.
If his promises were enough,
I'll liken them to a dance, turning
and returning its precise pirouette.
On a dance floor your two slippered feet
imagining the man's moist whispers
were of happiness or love.
But if his promises failed,
I'll surround the dance floor
with its hotel, where you woke
around midnight with him
at the foot of your bed. Pathetically
his head lifted off the quilt.
Then he left abruptly. The night for him
had been one long, intentional mistake.
You woke again at two
to the regularity of your own breath
and the darkening voices of that last dream
in which you ran over a young cellist's hand,
then casually drove away.
Switching on the nightstand light, you recognized sounds
sifting through the walls from a couple next door.
It was 3 a.m.

Somewhere in Texas there was a gloved wrist
with a whip so quick it snapped caps
off the necks of coke bottles, a hat off the head
of a balding man. Or so you once told me.
You stood waiting for some kind of finale, some kind
of release, until the wrist chose a woman.
The whip snapped once, before flinging out
to coil around her small waist.
That wrist could do anything, you said.
It could hold a promise to a promise
or slice a man's neck wide open

if that promise failed.
It could threaten or impress
or even force affection by pulling
the woman to that wrist and mouth
in a hundred dizzying pirouettes.

I've begun again with a French countryhouse
in northwestern Pennsylvania of white-washed brick,
red-trimmed windows, a slate roof.
It is three hundred miles from the ocean, but a breeze
blows through here from a lake nearby,
and the breeze brings with it a slight scent
of salt, so you could think
you were only a block from the beach,
where, imagined by a young girl in the house,
the smells of steamed hot dogs and beer
mingle with the musk of suntan oil,
bodies sprawling in the sun, the tangled
lust of their summer's afternoon.
Or perhaps the salt-smell is from two horses
grazing in a pasture a few hundred feet north
of the house, their wiry tails
switching methodically each haunch
to ease their trouble with flies.
They were ridden hard this morning,
the saddles still outlined in dried sweat
on their backs. But I remember
I've begun again with the childhood house.
It is August and hot;
and, outside the house, gnats are pestering
the mother and father who are sunning themselves
this Sunday afternoon on their perfect lawn,
surrounded by roses and elephantine rhododendron
and a privet that opens out on the west side
to a corn field, that itself opens out to meandering
mountains, brought low and smooth by time, the
      Alleghenies.

The father is reading Baudelaire, and the mother,
program notes of last night's opera.
While from the house comes the agitation
of a mismanaged Scarlatti. Fran has brought her harpsichord
with her this time and promises to stay for a week.
And so the young girl and Fran sit side by side
at her harpsichord, playing the afternoons
long into night. The girl's chestnut-colored hair
is long and drapes the higher octaves
as she fingers the lower reaches of the keyboard.
Fran smiles approvingly, occasionally suggesting
which marked trills to accentuate, which
to ignore. Then Fran plays, her black skin
in the late afternoon heat glistening
the sweat of making the impossible
appear easy. Her short
chubby fingers choosing which notes,
then seeming to lengthen with each resounding phrase,
the way my memory of her lengthens—
details signifying a whole, scenes against scenes—
as if an entire life were just a series of fragments,
disjointed, cut-off, then pasted together:
brittle fibers corded and combed, a rope,
its midsection fraying where once touched
by a now unseen hand.

Basement light folds into itself.
And I find myself in another basement with you,
one untuned harpsichord, a stringless
mandolin, and an old side saddle.
Though I can barely see you for the light,
I can make out the shape of a finger
tracing the dusty creases of leather.
Then, lifting the lid of the harpsichord,
you manage Scarlatti
like a rumor that has lost its edge.
Headlights sweep the basement,

dividing ceiling from floor,
darkness from light.
The malignant cells dividing within you
were as close as you got to understanding
what now grows within me.

This early morning I think again of you, Fran,
and as the moon seems unwilling to punch its way
through fattened clouds, I think
I am as close as I can get—for now—
to understanding what you must have imagined
for three long years. Forgive me
for everything I have said that is untrue in order
to reinvent you. I wish I could tell you
of a morning at some distant breakfast
and of my son asking about a brightness
he has caught just behind my eyes.
His hand will reach up toward mine,
and I will say to him, "Listen
to the toy trumpets of Scarlatti at our window,"
though it is only a kiss of birds.
But I will say, "Can you hear the Scarlatti at the window?"
And he will look up at me, accepting anything.

I won't accept the photographs
or any other easy memory of you.
Instead, as I stand in the musty odor of splintering hemp,
I can't help one last remembrance—a train ride, cars
tunneling their way into your city.
It was to be my last journey toward you.
I can't help all the flowers or a stubborn last expression—
your bottom lip protruding.
Alone in one pew I shuffled
old snapshots of you at your harpsichord.
So your hands move across that keyboard,
even now as I hear a recording

of that same Scarlatti.
Something about the rise and precision
of each passing note, recorded, locked in,
will always bring to mind freedom or escape.
The last phrase lifts away, after birth,
a transparent rope connecting idea to object,
spirit to flesh, then to now.
A last phrase, and the voices of that frayed,
final E chord, persisting
in the brief, sudden harmony
of all that is left to make that music
that is the between, that is us.

Inheritance

Moment by moment light unwinds itself
from the harbor masts, and we find ourselves
collapsing into history. Dusk,
boats toss and fret
along the wooden quay.

Monuments to history
bound so, each to its piling, they are boats
by context not definition. Like pearls chained
on their fragile string. Like the tersely knit syllables
of an impossible idea.

I'm bent to the familiar slip
of a knot in the sea-drenched air.
I speak, but I fear there is no you
to listen. Moments succeed each other, invisible
on an endless line.

As I lug an ice chest to my patient Ford,
the sky takes on shapes
of the ancients' imaginings:
endless revisions of light.

If we were gods and could choose our inheritance,
mine would be water not the stars.
Its eternal music of lisp and spill.
Its regular soft collapse. The edge-edging against the shore:
definition by subtraction.
That it will take away is all I care to know.

Two:

A Two-Spoked Wheel:
Lyrics to the Deaf Composer

Bedřich Smetana (1824–1884) was the first truly important Bohemian nationalist composer. Considered the founder of Czech music, he is best known for his opera, *The Bartered Bride*, his series of symphonic poems, *Má vlast (My Country)*, and his string quartet, *From My Life*. As a result of syphilis, the composer became increasingly ill and lost his hearing completely. Finally, after suffering from great mental confusion and instability, Smetana entered the Prague Asylum where he died in 1884.

1. Serenade

The score of your *Bartered Bride*
sits on my piano's rack, its libretto
dog-eared and marked up with my brother's
familiar script. He once told me
he would have liked to compose
an opera without plot or lyric—
voices singing pure sound, heroines
with no history.
How many times must he have moved
his way through this score, its voices singing
of lives comfortably distant from his own?

With you one hundred years dead,
I question what is missing
from the pages I've read. Who was it
that escorted you from your home
that final time, bundled you in a squirrel coat,
your three children and the attendant
looking on in frightened approval?
I've read the deafness had caused
a loss of mind, that your last days were spent
gazing from a barred, tenth-storey window.
Since no one came to visit the dying
so-called founder of Czech music,
who were the voices
that spoke to you on your deathbed?
Was there talk of a heaven or a hell?
Smetana, can I compose a history of you
without you?

My brother loves you
and returns to your music
from his own hospital room.
His record of *The Bartered Bride*
is worn, the arias scratched,
the heroine, Marie, still pining
for an impossible love.

Does your deafness and its consequent lyric
speak to him of what is irreparable,
or what can distance the self
from the shadow of self?
Are heroes only habits
for people beyond hope? Or for my brother,
who listens to your opera,
as he looks at his face in the metal
hospital mirror, the same face that asks
"Who are you?," then lathers up—
but no razor with which to shave.

2. *Pianissimo*!

(Prague: Konvikt Hall, 1984/1874)

Glancing at my wristwatch, I consider
where I am and where I am not—
suddenly captured by a flock of strings,
the preened collars and ruffled tails
of an audience, seats
now sagging under the weight of dumplings.
A gong tells me the night is prepared:
an expectant flutter, rustle, warm-up,
the wail of catgut slowly increasing.

So this is how we meet:
I simply find you in the seat beside me.
I recognize the eyes
that in this dimmed light
seem to look everywhere
but where they are looking.
And I know the flat crack
of your catarrh interrupting the music,
and bending toward me the familiar whispers:
"If only I could hear one note
of the thousand I have composed."
Then you're standing,

moving through the muted light
and the quiet of the movement
noted *pianissimo*. The heavy embarrassment
of your walk, its squeak and thud
through the breathless hall.
Not one head turns.
The lamps dim, the audience
no longer listens—
and you're gone,
the concert droning on without its god.

3.

Last night from a dream:
a drawing room, a woman, and you.
It was a night of phrases scribbled
because she had to speak
to you that way.

You were at your pianoforte,
studying a score of the *Kiss*,
an off-key song rising
in your throat, so unaware of itself,
innocent of sound.
Though I've read you had no sister,
you have a sister here.
As you sing, her back
to you, she scribbles then turns,
and she is naked.
There are a few small, dark moles
on both breasts.

I will want to remember her whiteness
and your astonished face. And to tell you
of the glass my own brother
once shattered across my record
of your final string quartet—*From My Life*—

19

the pieces of glass, his trembling hands,
my inability to save anything then.
The power I hold
when able to help
or not help.

Turning first to return
a key to its father clock, she leaves.
As I now turn to feel your hands
around my waist, to steal her shadow,
her figure, and all regret.

4. Turn/Counterturn, 1860

It is Göteborg, the year of her death.
You step to greet me
from a doorway that never mattered before.
From something I've read I recognize the room
with its covered piano like a linen ghost,
its dusty teacups and servers and skirts
of old curtains. As you take my hand
you tell me of her visit and illness.
Promising her recovery,
you suggested she leave.
And on the train home she died.
You tell me she is, even now, walking with us,
the sister you could never hold again.
I tell myself, *There was nothing*
he could have done. She would have died regardless.
I feel a memory glancing off my shoulder
when you say, "What kind of heaven
would you have if you knew that someone you loved
was in hell?" *And what*, I think,
if that someone is yourself?

*

You play for me.
On and on you play, while through the walls

drift the years and a few distant notes
from Mother's Bechstein, a tap running,
a pen scratching. I admit
this is all of heaven that I know.
I imagine that, after taking
his pre-dinner valium,
my brother must still be listening to *The Bartered Bride*
on the hospital verandah.
I will always remember the bouganvillea there
and, as a child, his delicate expression
of indifference as he greeted me.
He was twenty, an incomprehensible age
to me, at ten. I'd come,
he thought, to save him from
the endless therapy of revision.
He was tall, too thin; his room,
too bare and simple, or my memory of it
is simple: a cot, a suitcase,
a washstand, its metal mirror, a phonograph,
a worn record of *The Bartered Bride.*
That white day twenty years ago
or rather, one hundred and twenty from now, Smetana,
my brother will play the opera for me,
as you play a piece of it now
into the night, until the room
blushes red, until I rise, leaving only space
where for a time we sat together.

5. At *The Bartered Bride*

Turn to me, Bedřich, and see
my whispers in this Great Hall of Prague,
where we've come to see your opera.
Somehow the facts get skewed;
it was you who went deaf.
Beethoven, I love him, too.
But he never heard the shattering

21

of that strident high E, as you did —
like my brother's screams
that would wake him to silence
and falling snow. Sometimes you still
think you hear the last migratory sparrow, fading.

Then what holds you here? Opera glasses
to check the movements of strings?
Tracing a beautiful ear, you rest
one finger on its lobe as if you might
hear the lyric. Everyone knows this *Bartered Bride*,
but how many would know you as I do?
Won't you hear these last few trills? —
old leaves rolling their tongues, the swallows
turning south? Your ability to hear
without hearing; was this, then, your nobility?

6.

So you turn to me and say,
"Today I saw a leaf wobbling from its otherwise
barren limb, as a perfect trill will turn in
upon itself then skip to its surrounding notes.
And I saw harvesters swinging their sickles.
I pretend I can hear them
on their way home through twilight, the women
throwing off scarves and laughing.

For me, a bird dropping from its tree
is the descent of all sound;
so all motion is music.
I stand again at the edge of that field
where notes from a flute
lured me to travel beyond
the woods I had just visited, beyond the eye
like a scared astronomer

who still sees through his cracked lens—
Saturn on a blank canvas.

When I stepped into that field,
I heard harps, then the flourish of Liszt's
'Mephisto Waltz,' then that stinging high E
in my inner ear, then nothing—
the flat white of no sound.

This is how I translate sound from silence.
But it is necessity, not nobility, I speak of."

7. At the Planetarium

A starlit ceiling.
Mother's claustrophobia has left me alone
in this planetarium's dark night with you,

a figure from my night asking me
to identify the Ninth Sea.
I hesitate.

You turn away,
questioning what I already know:
nine paths circling atoms, nine planets,
nine symphonies . . . nine seas?

So the frontiers are not what I thought?

How do I define these figments
of my own imagination? Mr.Smetana?

You are my Ninth Sea,
the poem that writes itself
on a dreamlit wall.

Am I responsible for you, too,
oh my scared astronomer who first sees
beyond his shattered lens
and through the eye of that one star, hanging
before us on its slit black nerve—

a *tenth* planet on a blank canvas.

8. Convalescence, 1875

"I trace my days
in nets of sunlight
entangling light in light.
At first I thought only of open sky,
birds stretched across it,
summer fields with wheat
disappearing in even stitches
over the next low hill, as smooth
as your chestnut-colored hair.

The inventory of my days
is the inventory of this simple room:
wooden chair, porcelain bowl, cot,
no pen: I think incessantly of keys.

With oiled cotton plugging my ears I count
and count again anything countable—
grains in wood, lines in my own skin,
the letters unwritten to you, Julia.
I know these are prisoner's thoughts
as I await my cure.

And you? And your self-made winter
in Prague? Do you still sit in the afternoons
sipping sassafras tea, writing about a life
you can't possibly lead?
I am not the fiction

for whom you are responsible. Julia,
you've turned to me to understand
what makes a man at once hideous and beautiful.
Look at the syphilitic sores on my hands
then tell me, who would want a world
that is genderless, perfect?"

9.

I searched for a little nobility today,
so I read a book about you.
My Smetana, it was syphilis
that made you deaf, then mad,
then killed you. Toward the end
from your hospital bed,
you babbled to Liszt, Beethoven and Wagner
to share your bleached
and insignificant last hours.

Wearying, I put down the book,
venturing out to walk along the Elbe.
I found a young woman strolling along the riverbank
after-hours. Her mascara was smudged,
and she was smoking. She had rolled down
her seamed stockings to her ankles.
All I had wanted
was a little nobility.

Returning home, I picked up another book,
Czechoslovakia Since 1940,
read about Nemec, a member of your Czech
philharmonic. He had written
an article in 1945
defending *Má vlast,* and they beat him, Smetana,
to chants of "Heil Hitler!" they beat him to death.
I asked myself, if you had been alive then,
what would you have done, what would I?

But you're no twentieth century man.
I can't love you as Nemec,
or my brother, or your imagined sister did.
I threw down the book, still craving
my little nobility and went into the bathroom,
realizing you'd never be home—and all you had done
was seduce me from myself.

In the three-sided folding mirror,
in that triptych of myself, I saw at last
that to make the record complete,
I must begin to cry for myself,
for all that I owe, not a heaven, but myself.

10.

He returns to me today.
It is Autumn, mid-October
to be exact. My brother
will soon be forty.
Another season in its passing.
After thirty years
I still don't understand a life
so nervous with color, celebrating
its own demise.
It is an old theme.

As we walk the countryside today
my brother tells me of his life now,
how he grows attached to motel rooms
because there is nothing in them.
Strange cities are kind to him,
he tells me, anonymous and kind.
He photographs buildings now,
their geometries, patterns
that translate black and white.
They are a source of inspiration to him.

He wants to be close to me,
but the latest tragedy, the wrong
of a single life, is not much more to me now
than a single leaf's descent,
its one lazy descent, so graceful,
at peace with itself, as if it at last
understood its origins.
Or the way light folds into itself
this time of year, just a little cruel,
a little distanced like an old prayer.
So our lives fall away from ourselves
and each other, becoming too complicated
to hold onto for long.
I will also let go of you,
after your wide hand pulls me toward you
in this cruel hospital light
for a kiss
that could last centuries.

11.

Outside your hospital room,
the nurses with their odd winged caps
and opaqued-white legs zipping past
look quizzically at me.
I must seem out of place in my denim skirt
and clogs amidst this 19th century clatter—
medicine bottles rattling in their hurried carts,
the squeal of rusty stretcher wheels,
these overcrowded, noisy halls, dark, impenetrable.

I knock, then enter without invitation.
The room is quiet, dimmed.
My friend, though you have not recognized
anyone for a month now, our unspoken intimacies
hover above the dingy bedclothes,
above the lingering smells of blood

and urine. Your translucent eyes are fixed
on the bright ceiling lamp,
as if the source of all things burned there.
What do you see? You with your matted
and graying hair, now grown past your shoulders,
its musty smell mixing with all the other
excretions of your own mortality.
But it's no use.
You are to die in a week's time.

Your sheets are stained.
And as I stand at the foot of your bed,
another blossoming, I too hear
Liszt ranting just outside the window—strains of his
"Mephisto Waltz" through the walls as back-up—
Beethoven and Nijinsky, that handless
South American cellist, and anyone else
who ever defied against all odds
the gravitational pull toward despair.
I'll call you and all the mad
hopeless friends who have preceded
or followed you, each with his own despairing tale,
and your music, the burden
of its loss as each note decays into the next—
all of this I'll dare to call beautiful.

12.

There is beauty, too, in this:
the fact that little can be saved,
though everything is worth saving.
For instance, a record skips
and skips. Memory hitches,
skips a beat,
then settles on this: 1965. The bathroom door,
left unlocked. From inside
the whine of an old faucet, its valve opening,

tapwater running, the smooth water
on my tired skin. Through the walls
drift a few distant notes,
Mother's Bechstein. The latch clicks open.
My brother's face moves
toward tonight's bath water.
I think knowledge is no more
than the words, "I want you,"
and the girl's, my fear
of them ever being true. The echoes
that reach me now, my brother's knuckles
rapping the tub's edge.
The shock of his words, then his hands.
I imagine sores on his slender fingers
but say, "How lovely."

Smetana, if not flawed
how do we dare exist?

13. Sympathy Pains

My brother grows younger, loving the rain.
He loves waking to mornings
smelling of the sea, to the washed-out pallor
of sky, and the familiar hiss of a slick
city street—like an evaporation of anger,
a moist language rising to his window—
so unlike the calm
of that same street muted
three months later by snow.

From the hospital's tenth floor window,
a dream of distance, a prayer
to the street below.
My brother sits on the edge of his bed,
praying into cupped hands.
The rain exhausts itself
against the glass.

*

He tells me he could say "clock" at two,
could tell time at three, and was aware of its passing
at four. At five, the playground girls,
twirling and laughing around him,
their skirts flying up in his face,
were just little girls; even the one,
hooking him with the questionmark of a finger,
then pulling him to the back of the schoolhouse
to dawdle limp panties in his face
until he screamed, turned his back on her,
his face to a blank wall. *I tell you*
it's not easy to spend the night with ice
tinkling in its glass and particles of thought
pinging off the walls like electrons.
My conscience is bothered by inactivity.
My conscience is a two-spoked,
numbered wheel that would like to turn
the colors of my imagination off.

He talks on.
I watch people pass on the street below,
their sex obscured by mist.

*

I imagine that wheel can spin backwards.

From Rome one year
Brother wrote of the Colloseum
and crowded buses, of the beautiful
young men. From Berlin
he wrote of the blue permanence of sky,
of a Mahler dirge he had wept over,
played by a small string ensemble at the Berlin Wall.
The boundaries that separate the love of one man
for another; this was his divided world.
And from Amsterdam the letters were of rain,
of waterfront mornings, of thick warm beer, mackerel
and brie he would eat in the evenings

at a favorite café.
His days were like dominoes lined up,
while he waited for a wind to do
what his own hand wouldn't.
He would imagine himself smaller
while images rushed at him,
enormous, out of reach: the midnight streets
of Amsterdam, the unforgiving
December air, overturned carts, their rotting produce
spilled onto the street, the insistent rain like petals
discarded from a cloud. He would hardly know
what to admit to himself,
or what the soul is composed of —
just a little night. Or that the night
could be a woman unbuttoning her blouse
behind dusty venetian blinds,
as a strand from a flute
threads its way from her window to the street.
He knows only that the rain becomes him;
how it suffers its fallings
and risings as it begins
to lift off the steamy sidewalks
for the first time in weeks.

*

That wheel spins back even farther.

As children we once walked the boundaries
of an abandoned farm in Vermont.
Our parents remained with the picnic at the car.
We walked in silence, glancing occasionally
at a bowing old willow, or a crumbling trellis
still choked with clematis.
The barn, too, was ruined, no clues left
of the story of what was whole and strong
before it was ended.
I imagined the young boy who might have lived here,
whose hands one harvest ached
from the hundreds of lifted bales, the twine's

deep imprint across his palms,
who one afternoon walked out
into the sunlight, swinging buckets of milk.
In an hour or two the barn was gone, consumed—
by a careless match a workhand might have tossed
onto the virgin hay. And with the flames came birds
escaping through the slats, the animal
hysteria. I was afraid
to ask what histories
my brother conjured from the barn,
what thoughts we might rebuild it with.

*

Last evening on my way to the hospital, I saw
an old man on a streetcorner
waving and jabbering nonsense
to all the passing cars.
It was sad, this talk to no one. Maybe
he remembered years ago,
a lover saying goodbye to him
and he, waving and gesturing to her,
as he gestured now.
Maybe they were meant for a mother or a son,
those huge hands flailing
at the pale evening sky. Or just maybe
their wild movement was a desperate act
directed to any god who would listen,
an act as desperate as my brother's
the day he struck out to our barn
and lit the match and placed
it on the tender hay as before an icon.
Something that sounds like prayer:
new flames crackling around him.
The dim golden light of a thousand candles
compared to this. Later,
the lies he told us, the denial,
the truth fallen back, like my blindfolded mare
who reared back into the flames.

*

His hospital room
is as still as a forest
in winter. No birds fly overhead,
no indications of promise or return.
Only a cloudless white ceiling
and a poor sun.

A young girl's voice from the next room.
I could imagine her in a red dress
smoking a long brown cigarette
or slipping out of that dress
and into a brother's arms —
But I won't.
Or I could bring that composer back,
as if to close the centuries, the distance between
my brother and me.
But music makes nothing happen.

I had wanted to take a composer's notes
then describe birds in flight,
a fractured angel's wing falling
onto damp earth.
I could have imagined anything for my brother,
and he would still be here in this hospital,
and Smetana would not. I could have walked
into his small world and told him
that had the composer lived now,
he could have been saved, a simple injection,
a few drugs. I know that.
And I know that my brother
is my brother, and is as he is.
So little on this damp earth
we can do. And small room for pity,
everlastingness being little more
than a few pure,
imperfect eighth notes
slipping from a pen.
As when we sometimes speak —

too much heart and not the right words—
so in the face of people we could love
we are only invisible drums
pounding and pounding
to an audience of one.

Three:

Familial Present

Husband, As If a Brother

I could tell you lies
of the flesh, but I won't.
Nights, after the breasts
have been touched and touched,
I rise from our arched postures of desire
then loss and return to the room
where I try to cleanse whatever doubts
I may have. Some moments
you are too familiar.
So I extend them precisely, counted and parcelled,
keeping track so you won't miss me
too long. This is the secret of my deceit,
the impossible hush of my sexual self,
which I wrap in an auburn towel,
so I won't have to look
at the sad thing I've become
over and over. Water flushes,
blossoming in the toilet. I tell you this
out of love.

And of the darker circles of my youth
I know this: there were no centers,
only the concentricities of guilt,
forever widening. As if each touch—
even yours—could carry with it
a history of shame—he
who should not have touched,
touching first.

Sometimes the Body's Unwilling

Something in the heat of this afternoon
reminds me of murder.
The evening news confirms: two homicides,
three suicides, and one arson—"accidental,"
or so the convicted assures us.

Forgive me, my world:
I feel treacherous and abandon
what I most love. Or it abandons me,
the way men in white sweaters
dragging the lake for an unidentifiable body
will give up around midnight,
returning home.

Believe me, I never planned it this way:
Love taking off her blue slippers;
I have become too much for her.
I'm tired of counting stars
that lie hidden like tiny fists
just behind my eyelids.
In sleep, razors
carve rhythms from my short, nervous breaths,
as a flower is carved by some gentler hand.

Listen, tomorrow
I will go to the shore,
lie flat on my back with one eye cracked,
and watch clouds slipping by me
like children, lost and amazed.

Possibilities

I think the day will outlast you.
Another line preceded this,
though it was afraid to take off
its pale dress, to slip under the sheet
with the terrible stain.

I could think of trains and desire.
Of a bird's cold throat
as one long note, descending an oak,
fisted and threatening its sky.
Or of this morning as I watched faint pictures
on a screen, and the doctor's voice:
"Yes it is there. And the small ocean around it."
I wanted to correct, say *he* is there.
Say *yes, of course, his ocean.*

If this is loneliness—measurement
and study, your ghost on a screen, tomorrow
stilled and senseless—then loneliness *is* the face
of a child.

From the oak the bird sings throatlessly.
I won't trust the sound of it or any promise
on a screen, looking mostly like a face
in a subway window
disappearing down that cold tunnel

toward night. And the opposite of night:
what pushes the cars forward, naked
and unafraid.

No Apology

Now I resist all photographs.
Particularly the one of you
taken in 1970: you're leaning
against a wall on some backstreet
in Memphis, scrawls in black & red above you:
"Found in the crime of passion
is the crime of love." In that one
you're twenty-four and smiling
at your executioner—that's me—
the shutter slicing you off
at the neck. Or the other one
from Atlantic City, 1978, a Panama hat
shading your face, the afternoon tide
rising behind you. Only hours before
you had startled awake
then lit a candle at our bedside
to make sure I still was beside you.
You would soon be gone,
and with one frame left
I wanted it to be of you
boarding the train, your hat tipped,
your wave tentative, your uniform smartly pressed.
Once again the camera clicks,
as if our motions of return, from symbol to act,
artifice to moment, could be found
in such small gestures of black & white.
I know you were right that day in Atlantic City
as we sprawled in the sun
tracing the seam that was horizon separating
light from water, water from
what you told me:
that the pictures of your family, the one
of your mother and father shucking peas
on the patio would not keep her young
or your father alive. Or another
unable to freeze your brother's
young legs linked through yours

as you tell your stories to the night,
to him who would a few years later
die a young soldier.
Or another: your arms ten years later linked
through a wife's, through the arms
that were not mine, the two of you
swirling all night on a dance floor
to some dixie tune. Or the arms
linked much later through mine,
as we survey our garden
in the face of a summer of regrets,
knowing that what's left
of the softening tomatoes
will be nipped tonight,
knowing that the process of loss
proceeds unhindered
with little record or return.

Disclosures

An absence of leaves long fallen
discloses a world we think
we never guessed was there.
Tucked into woods we find the unremarkable:
a weathered shed, a small red glove
lost to snow, a neighboring house,
its red shutters thrown wide.
Somehow we're now more convinced
of our small world, as if things don't exist
until we're sure they're there,
as if a playing card, face down,
could be any suit or value until rolled.
This morning over coffee and cigarettes,
we listen to the highway
through the stripped November branches—
hurried engines grinding toward work.
Closer in, the panic of migrating birds,
the dry-throated rasp
of branch on branch, the shortness of breath
in the language between us.

*

While our marriage remains
the pentimento of the seen
and almost seen, the heard and almost heard,
the little we disclose to one another
is hardly worth the mention.
What we wanted to say
becomes distorted, modified beyond recognition
in the telling or not telling.
Our actions, a poor portraiture; our words,
translations into an easier tongue
that help us to get through each successive day
together. So the suitcase
hidden in the closet

stays hidden, while the sun keeps straining
toward another end, pricked by the branches
that rise from the southwest corner of our dormant wood.

*

What is left, my hardly tangible Love?—
a portrait of you in winter.
Midmorning. Dressed in plaid,
you're chopping wood.
The new axe glints
like a semaphore mirror.
But there's no message in the axe.
If I thought there were,
I'd wait, as messenger,
by our frost-glazed window
pen in hand, until the distance
between intent and disclosure
closes, and our world collapses
to a few lights in a house,
to the frost-blurred silhouette of a woman
bent over her sink, to the tired scrape and shuffle
of familiar steps, and a gloved hand at the door
offering something tangible,
like wood.

Hatteras

The Cape, midsummer.
The waves continue to ruin themselves
against the shore in their long definition
of boundary and ownership, like the pronouns
with which I attempt and usually fail
to possess what is
and still what can never be mine:
my husband, my child,
my dog, my self, the dulled edge
of my understanding, and so on.

It is the wrong time of day
with no moon to stamp
the water ethereal.
Just the mutable arcs
of wave on wave, the luckless birds
and the high-noon sun. The shadow
of a single mottled cloud moves in,
dulling the brilliant sand,
and it rains awhile.

Which gives me time to consider the morning,
when I could not identify the hard-won fish,
belly-up on the deck of our boat,
the fishhook piercing one gelatinous eye.
If not already dead,
the fish was surely blinded.
So I threw it back,
as if I could not possess
what I could not name or heal.
For my boy, just one, learning to dream
on the cabin's steamy cushions, these thoughts,
a string of half-formed consonants on a sleepy tongue.

The rain lifts, the shadow passes.

My son is not yet old enough to care about
weather. Nor does he know
that he has yet no name for *earth, moon,
despair*. And a small understanding.
At the edge of water this is what matters:
he lifts his palms and arms as if
to hug his near-nameless world,
and it is his in that *as if*.

Duet in the Suburbs

The telephone rings and you answer it.
It answers back with
silence on the other end. Holding on
you imagine beginnings and endings
of worlds:

You and the man you live with
have an argument over a moot point.
You hear only the discussion's
harsh syllables, fragments
of a more complete sound,
as if just now
you are inventing words.

It's spring,
and at this swollen time of year,
the lake closes in on your house.
In the afternoon you watch overalled men
lowering nets, hooks and grapples
into the water.
Something catches in your throat,
as the harrow's ribbons of steel
disappear below the surface.
When at five with nothing to show
the men haul the harrow
to a more distant point, you're glad
they couldn't find whatever body
you hope will remain inviolate,
silent and secure
among the reeds and rushes of the water.

Do you have a voice?
That night, fireside, you agree with everything
he says. He even changes
your opinion of water,
turning you toward wind, explaining
that panicked souls are swept
up in it to God. You admire
whips of forsythia
in a far corner of the room
that you've forced to bloom, just out of season.
Though you have trouble with god,
you admit a hymn from childhood sticks,
a hymn sung to your boy
when he'll listen.
The hymn is what
you have to pass on.

Today you care for the ephemeral,
knowing the forced
forsythia will likely
die in a week's time.
Without your knowing atoms split,
the world complicates itself, straining
toward the inert: leaves
in their helter-skelter descent,
bound to the old marriage
of gravity to wind.
Today is the beginning
of a love for what you can't
keep hold of.

The telephone rings, and you run
to answer it. This time, a voice, formal
and unfamiliar. A sickening *thunk*
from the next room. Panicked,
you drop the phone and run;

your child has fallen from his high chair.
He's shocked into silence,
though his little fingers are frantic,
as if articulating
the scream that suddenly issues
from your throat,
the voice you had thought
was inviolate, secure.
Sometimes it takes years
between impact and reaction.
Then the birth into language
is as terrifying as silence
or love.

Caress

For a time before you left
I wanted to believe
that I was indestructible.

The sun was my private metaphor
for consistent irrefutable return.
Not the real sun, but the one

carefully etched into the porcelain jar
that shared the space on my mantel
with a glass figure of a horse

and a solid gold Tiffany clock.
On the jar the slim figure of a girl
extending her arms upward, as if to touch

the brightness. At the time I didn't know metaphor
belongs to everyone and is mutable
in that—from the pen of another

the sun is no longer
what I say it is. What returns now
is an angry moment beyond anyone's control

when the jar went spinning
to the floor and shattered—I thought
how like the possible destiny of a small planet.

The long moments
between touch and break
were compressed into a single need to remember.

At what moment did I lose sight of the sun?
Who was to blame?
When was it my body lost sight of itself

as whole, as if it, not the jar, had chosen
to break? After the jar fell,
your eyes filled

with scattered light, looking off
toward an end. The pieces
were like dancers who fall away

from their faltering dance yet remain on stage,
as fragments, individually perfect
in their fall. Everything is metaphorical

though not necessarily mine.
A string of consonants and vowels extends the room's
finite space. Then comes

the sudden, irreversible knowledge:
how delicate the hand that broke the jar,
how terrifying its touch,

almost too fragile to be human.

Love Poem

On the flat slate,
in relief, is an ancient code
of a waning sea
composed the last time
the tides went out
tens of millions of years ago.
My sweet geologist,
under our night sky,
desperate for what matters and what lasts,
you hunched over a slab
of what helps puzzle together
our back patio,
that stone that is
beyond the both of us.
You traced the water's curved grace
and movement, the sequence
of parallel rippling lines
captured as stilled weight
and permanence; even so,
the water's signature smudging
to dust as we spoke.
The pink shock
of azalea, this year
shading the piece of rock,
bleeds through any
absence of light.
We move from shadow
to shadow in the long arc of days
that cannot tally more than this:
our enduring gifts, if we're lucky,
a single blistered leaving,
a single curve;
this must be love.

Four:

Individually

Entropy

It all comes down
to so little:
the startled lightning,
its release, the flood
that leaves several families
stranded in a neighborhood,
distant from our sympathies,
a neighborhood we casually hear about
on the six o'clock news.
But haven't distance and rain always
made us merciless, the way they both
deny light? And hasn't
whatever order there is
always been blurred
by our own small world of ink
and its momentary sadnesses?

The rain settles,
becoming a formal occasion,
while the laundry we have neglected
to collect shudders abandoned on its line.
And as the azaleas' middle-aged blossoms
are stripped from their branches,
an order becomes clear again—
just patches of falling color
blurred by rain.

From some disturbance of sleep
over which we have no control,
our children are waking in adjacent rooms,
terrified of the lands they've just travelled,
the rock just trapped in
like a sculptor's uneasy image
of his unformed art.
We can only comfort them with words,
as the light from the overloaded moon
competes with the light from the ghoulish faces

of their Mickey Mouse lamps, and they fall back
into a different sleep. They will wake
to a poverty of first morning light
(its dim boundaries) and will remember nothing
of the orderless night they managed
to sleep and not sleep through,
their collective memory hurtling
toward a future as yet unformed,
as yet merciless in its small comforts,
as it nestles into its dreamless sleep.

Hair of the Dog

> "There is here no measuring with time, no year matters,
> and ten years are nothing." —Rainer Maria Rilke

The sun squints against mid-summer's heat.
Lounging outside, my pores are loosening
last night's debauchery.
Most of my women friends are unhappy
loving the men they love,
compelled as they are in their unhappiness,
as if in love lies the tally
of all possible measure and scope.
Ice in my glass, I am momentarily promised
to a figurative sea. No lifeboats
on the nearly-clear waters of peppered vodka,
bound in by glass and air.
Outside the glass, where there has been
no rain for weeks, the trees
are unsteady in a promiseless wind.
The new yet brittle leaves
tear easily or are ditched
like a scant half-realized idea of love.

Having lived each sober day
as if completely dimensional, parcelled
into the perfect white squares of a desk
blotter calendar, I long for no boundaries.
Hungover, I lose a sense of depth and shape;
the day is full of promise.
Long shadows cross and cross
invading, engulfing the distant hills.
They reaffirm the random movements
of gulls, not of time.

Another vodka, and the day fills with an absence:
the just perceptible lilt of an empty backyard swing
hitched to my garden's tallest tree.
There is shape to the space where the child is not
and a hidden gift of sudden measurable laughter.

No hint of sorrow, the absent astronaut
of the garden halves her space,
giving what is otherwise formless
a form. The long arc of the rope's
sure path, like that of the elegant brass arm
of a grandfather clock, dividing, dividing
what is neither visible, nor barely divisible
in this world.

Possibly So

This morning, just a few feet
from my kitchen window, from out of the otherwise
dark woods, a patch of solitary light.
The donors of shadow,
five or six larch trees, framed
that pocket of light, the way long hair will
a lovely face. The handful of light
remained, as a remarkable dream
will remain with its dreamer, though the hills
the dreamer tried repeatedly to climb
may grow steeper with distance
on the dream and his stunning sky,
a little dimmer, less profound.
But for this dreamer
the ground just under the light
was radiant, as if lit from beneath, or as if
some long-forgotten god were trapped
under the earth, wanting above all to be freed.
His anxious, failing breath condensing
into gold light. His wings
clipped long ago.

Hypersomnia: Exhaustion After a Long Night's Rest

There is a sleep from which some people never fully awake,
a sleep in which they first dream
hurriedly at dawn of a lake
for which they shadow-write
ghost lilies vying for substantial air,
old bodies of trees parcelling the green-misted water,
once felled, to be abandoned by half-starved beavers.

They, the unwaking, could make anything happen—
the lilies could become them,
their long arms languishing.
Or the trees could take wing or swim toward a drier,
healthier ground. Or they could sleep on,
splicing the dream with yet another.
And this unrequited knowledge wakes them,
abandoning the possible.

Awake, they call the lake their miserable friend.
They call its waters metaphor for soul.
Whatever the name, it doesn't really matter.
Exhausted after rest,
they're confused by a mid-August poplar
beginning to give up its leaves.
Midday darkens, unidentifiable in its malaise.

The trouble is, they carry sleep with them,
like unnecessary baggage on the long train ride
from a to z when they travel
in a compartment marked "Restricted."
Tired rain blossoms on the promiscuous windowpanes.
They read history in it.

For You, Elizabeth

The orchard grew heavy. The days
shied away from blue. While the trees
held up prisms of light.

I think this is why
Tolstoi decided to make her blue.
At least I think it was Tolstoi
who put his Anna in blue,
in a blue ballroom, waiting
for a man who would never arrive,
a man who had already ridden off
on an old mare as far as Poland
for good. I say Tolstoi,
but it could be any of us.

Today, I woke to blue rain and statistics,
to the tragedy of radios
diminished to static,
until I got tired of statistics,
turned them off.
For an hour or more I lay there, hearing
hard little fists
of rain on the pavement. After that,
a kind of canon through the walls:
two voices crooning a song.
Her reply mimicking his,
then the precise crystalline clarity
of no reply at all.
I saw them shifting on sheets like sails,
him rising above her,
a St. Christopher medal or Star of David
falling against her small firm chest.
And for now I will call her Elizabeth,
because an Elizabeth is no one I know.
The man above her will remain nameless,
because he could be anyone I know.
Before I woke I dreamt of a similar man:

a Russian officer riding across Poland
on an afternoon hammered in sunlight.
In that dream I am
the sound of hooves coming up
from behind, the sound
of fifteen rounds pumped ruthlessly
into the officer's back
by a sergeant from Poland.
I *am* that Polish sergeant, gone mad.

Now I lie here listening through walls
like a priest, his one ear pressed
to the confessional's *cloison*,
allowing the unseen side to betray a life.
Each soft voice an Anna,
a Helen, a St. Theresa, or you,
Elizabeth, as if the prism of history
could reduce to a single tone
these voices in the dawn.
This is how I woke listening
to any man's history which is always
a fiction of the long struggle
against noise.

Gray

Often in early morning to some Beethoven or Brahms
a red bird arrives at my feeder,
while nearby my old gray cat
blends into bald branches—
not at all insistent or startling.
The two to me share a value in their equation of light:
the cat, the bird—cut-outs in snow
that exploit their little chance for breadth or depth
with an ever-measured distance between them.

Isn't this, after all, how it goes?—
a body comes to feed, is frightened
and flies away unfed.
Then at night red birds become gray
and develop transparent wings,
that pester the edge of our sleep,
that have no appetite for open sky,
but feed and feed.

Then morning arrives, bringing more snow.
The wet snow with its terrible weight
burdens the feeder. I estimate the thickness
covering untouched flaxseed and millet,
and once again my world is dimensional.
My cat has brought me a gift,
fluttering to the backdoor stoop.

From my study, mid-afternoon, I sit red-sweatered
with a late quartet winding down
like a late main-sequence star. I look out
to snow, to an absence of what
can become desperate in us,
can fly away.

Elegy

Across from where I live
there is a field
that slopes gently upward for a mile or so
until I can see no farther.
I've always supposed the field continues
beyond the assurance of vision,
and have even imagined a rigorous order
of trees there, the unseen field
planted and populated according to each season.
I've occasionally seen signs of a world beyond—
a few scarves of smoke unravelling above
the horizon of land. Today I think
I could wish for little more
than this late-winter field
where for brief moments there is an abundance
of most anything ever wanted—of love
or virtue or sweet memory—clinging
to the dulled-yellow March grass.

I admit there are times I've thought
this fancy preposterous
from my smaller world of detail and scope.
More often I wonder how anything
more simple or beautiful
than the stripped image of a field in March
could survive. The field
is a blank slate held up to the mind,
the way a stillborn might be held briefly
to the mother's breast,
as if indeed an instant is all it has.

Night Flight

You can never tell which words
will betray you.
If given a chance these words
might give themselves up of their own accord,
like today's tense sky delivering itself
of snow. But this is not a story
of words, but of a woman
who stands across the street,
illumined by snow, allowing herself this thought:
millions of white petals falling. I believe
she questions her desire for streetcorners
and a bus that has yet to come.

Tucked away, this two-pronged memory—a cathedral,
its thousands of crenelations
rising to a burnt-white sky,
to ranks of spires piercing the bellies
of swollen Münchener clouds.
The woman almost remembers her high heel staccato,
marble steps, a huge oak door
sighing open, almost hears the tormented gargoyles
scowling from their perches,
as if they were frozen at that moment
just this side of freedom.

For a time, from the dark of a pew
she studies oblique light
escaping through colored glass.
It fails. The arched vault,
the fluted granite walls give up
what little light they once held.
She finds herself slightly embarrassed
by this lack of light, and
thinking herself alone, she is startled—
a young man's rosary beads clicking

like a purse snapping open then shut
one of her long winter days in Berlin.
That day, ten years ago,
she sat half-naked on a dilapidated couch,
only half-listening to her man's
short angular phrases. He is sobbing.
With the click of a cigarette lighter
she is denying what we may never hear.
Or what we may. For there is yet another story
that stays hidden in a darkened apartment,
where her whispers once slid
over an officer's epaulettes,
where he took her hand and kissed it,
though perhaps would have preferred to kiss her mouth.
It is an old story of betrayal.
But who is the betrayer, who the betrayed here?

"Yes," she had whispered
over the officer's epaulettes,
"I have watched them closely.
I have seen your spouse and mine together
many times."

Kiss of hand. Click of heels
and jackboots leaving.

Rising from the couch, her man recalls
the officer's wife, how her raccoon stole
had tickled his bruised cheek,
her sunburnt lips had tickled.
Now the only sounds:
the clink of ginned ice,
a second hand, the woman's ring
pinging to the floor.
Then: a squad of boots approaching.
Voices. Threats. A fist hammering
at the front door.
As surely as a cartridge ticks in its chamber,
a cell door clicks shut,

and ten years later, a plane hatch closes.
But this is not, after all, a story of betrayal,
and Flight 409 from Munich to Brussels
to Boston finds our woman hemmed in again by language.
Two Serbs speak maybe about husbands
in a tongue that is unmusical and frightening.
For hours she watches a man across the aisle
study his passport as if a prayerbook.

Then the landing,
the tense shuffle of return.
Customs men smelling of fish
and deodorant. A suspicious question,
glances from passport to face.
She would like to tell them she is one American
who detests the still lives of cameras, the easy click
of personal tragedy. Instead
she turns to little cargoes of memory
on the luggage carousel and a desire
to deny what is hers. She wants
to return to her flat, tuck herself away
somewhere in Brookline, belongingless.
But no, she simply returns.
To her apartment's one uncovered chair.
To open a stiff paperback too hard, crisp pages
slipping to the floor like unused or forgotten prayers.

By now you may have forgotten me and the street
where I watch her breath take shape. The snow
falls and falls as if an end
to her tale or the world.
But it's not.
For this has been little more
than the story of a woman
and her sad lack of any faith
in herself. What she holds in one clenched fist
could be a few flakes she has managed to capture—
if only for an instant. Like another's faith
in a thimbleful of light.

Whatever it is, it is
the only secret she keeps
from me, from her otherwise perfect history
of crossings and doublecrossings.

I flick on the light, the street goes black.
The keys of my typewriter clack off a new title:
Espionage Love.

Her bus
may or may not arrive.

Stargazing

If the soul is lusterless,
a dark knot beating toward light,
then I must have one.
Tonight under a paling sky
peering through a telescope's keener eye.
First, the flickering mistakes
of fireflies, then the smearings of galaxies.
Haloes and stars,
languid afterthoughts.
Saturn lost to me till now,
articulate, ring on ring.
From our deck you teach me of the stars,
so that a knot in cedar wood
swirls like a nebula perceived
for the first time.
If the soul is like this,
like heaven's dusty remnants,
then perhaps it is at once
forgiven and damned
as it randomly circles inward and outward,
ill-formed or formless,
borrowing its light. Forgiveness.
I fear there is little
of that for me.
Sometimes I hear my words forming
without thought, as though whatever swirling inside
had already been extinguished,
and speech is all there's left
to burn a tenuous proof.
For how many years will I be heard?

Holding On To This World

I wish I could undo the afternoon
like the paper napkin
where I've hidden a few pale crumbs
for a favorite colorless bird.
Undo it and offer what I could.
Some stars appear to me, some fail.
Those I can point to and call my own,
I'll wrap in a silk handkerchief
that one day perhaps I'll remember,
hidden at the bottom of my dresser drawer.

What I divine in my world I hold onto
because it is of this world.
And so for a moment I fashion and hold fast
to a few sweet images: bees half-hidden
in the languid purple of wisteria,
the scent of hummingbirds
stitching soft trumpet to vine, white butterflies
unstitched and falling from dogwood.

For some I suppose these petals *are*
what they suggest:
winged and sputtery, escaping upward, away
from this body. But for me, petals
are finally petals and they fall,
exceeding nothing. Exceeding nothing,
what lies moist in my palm
can be stars with a little fancy
or just fine, as crumbs, without.

Inheritance: While Listening to Mozart

Today on my daily walk
I nearly bumped into a ring-tailed coon
on my country lane. Confused, panicked,
he skittered back & forth & back
a worn distance of thirty feet.
I kept my own distance as I knew I should.
His all nerves and movement wooed
my vision to a heap, stilled and bloody
at lane's end. His mate, no doubt, he'd found.
I could tell by his urgent pull toward the body,
the lessening space between them
a taut thread, an ache, a lyre,
a shipwrecked boat.

*

Always there is the problem of time,
how to fill it,
how to stretch it to fit the words
for sorrow or tragedy or love.

Mozart knew about time: it is the vessel
for all possible sound. He filled it
better than most.

*

Another boat rises out of the mist
of a past, not entirely my own.
Jonquils and tulips sway in a grey March breeze.
A dog barks. A child
dodges little helicopters of poplar seeds.
Red shutters thrown wide, a childhood house looming.
The house is a boat, waiting to take on cargo.

Mozart, liquid dreams taking form.
A childhood house, a fluid
architecture of time.

How to fill it now?
How to rub the words into right shapes,
thin enough to slide with ease
under the windows, thick enough
for meaning, after I've guessed
that in the deaths of our parents is only a hope
for the revisions toward truth
or beauty.

Ruined boats all, descending scales.

And in the blue eyes of self-orphaned grief
the bright flourishes of Mozart,
warming the windows,
will spill from the cracks in the glass.

Sparks, Maryland

The fire's song is indecipherable.
I know this, as I know how today
I heard Snow Geese moving south and thought of summer,
of everything I could not have.

This is one way to enter a world:
to study tufts of flame ascending the sooted
shoot of a fireplace
and think of home,
of everything home was not.

Unlike you, Love,
I've never learned how to lay the fire
correctly. Just sparks and no flame,
some smoke.

The iced truth at the heart of a flame,
stilled in memory: a brother's mouth on mine.
A truth like that, then its ash, my real desire:
to desire desire, to want innocently, without
a history of guilt. Sometimes,

before the moving and spending,
I look into your eyes, Love, and see a brother,
and my hardly perfect history incarnates itself,
leaps up hotly, consuming itself.
And sometimes I hate what I see:
feathered ardor, just consumed,
not ascending.
You are not responsible for this:
my near-ignorance of fire.

Though I inhabit the town always,
I only occasionally live,
as in dream, in the village of Sparks.

Julia Wendell was born in Warren, Pennsylvania, in 1955. She received a B.A. in English Literature from Cornell University, 1977, an M.A. in English and American Literature from Boston University, 1978, and an M.F.A. from the University of Iowa, 1982. Founding Editor of The Galileo Press, Ltd., she lives in Sparks, Maryland, with her husband, Jack Stephens, and their two children, John Logan and Caitlin.